Least Sandpiper

Published by schifferbooks.com

Semipalmated Sandpiper

Published by schifferbooks.com

Spotted Sandpiper

Published by schifferbooks.com

Stilt Sandpiper

Published by schifferbooks.com

Solitary Sandpiper

Published by schifferbooks.com

Pectoral Sandpiper

Published by schifferbooks.com

White-rumped Sandpiper

Published by schifferbooks.com

Sanderling

Published by schifferbooks.com

Dunlin

Published by schifferbooks.com

Short-billed Dowitcher

Published by schifferbooks.com

Semipalmated Plover

Published by schifferbooks.com

Piping Plover

Published by schifferbooks.com

Black-bellied Plover

Published by schifferbooks.com

Black-bellied Plover (Immature)

Published by schifferbooks.com

Greater Yellowlegs

Published by schifferbooks.com

Lesser Yellowlegs

Published by schifferbooks.com

Red Knot

Published by schifferbooks.com

Ruddy Turnstone

Published by schifferbooks.com

Willet

Published by schifferbooks.com

Whimbrel

Published by schifferbooks.com

American Oystercatcher

Published by schifferbooks.com

Hudsonian Godwit

Published by schifferbooks.com

Marbled Godwit

Published by schifferbooks.com

Wilson's Phalarope

Published by schifferbooks.com

Great Blue Heron

Published by schifferbooks.com

Green Heron

Published by schifferbooks.com

Black-crowned Night Heron

Published by schifferbooks.com

Yellow-crowned Night Heron

Published by schifferbooks.com

Little Blue Heron

Published by schifferbooks.com

Snowy Egret

Published by schifferbooks.com

Great Egret

Published by schifferbooks.com

Glossy Ibis

Published by schifferbooks.com

American Bittern

Published by schifferbooks.com

Least Bittern

Published by schifferbooks.com

Common Snipe

Published by schifferbooks.com

Sora

Published by schifferbooks.com

Clapper Rail

Published by schifferbooks.com

Horned Lark

Published by schifferbooks.com

Snow Bunting

Published by schifferbooks.com

Killdeer

Published by schifferbooks.com